patios
DESIGNS FOR LIVING

Meredith®
BOOKS

PATIOS DESIGNS FOR LIVING®

Editor: Paula Marshall

Contributing Editor: Catherine M. Staub, Lexicon Consulting, Inc.

Contributing Associate Editor: Julie Collins, Lexicon Consulting, Inc.

Contributing Writer: Martin Miller

Contributing Assistants: Bridget Nelson, Holly Reynolds, Megan Stotmeister, Lexicon Consulting, Inc.

Graphic Designer: On-Purpos, Inc.

Copy Chief: Terri Fredrickson

Publishing Operations Manager: Karen Schirm

Senior Editor, Asset and Information Manager: Phillip Morgan

Edit and Design Coordinator: Mary Lee Gavin

Editorial and Design Assistant: Renee E. McAtee

Book Production Managers: Pam Kvitne, Marjorie J. Schenkelberg, Rick von Holdt, Mark Weaver

Contributing Copy Editor: Nancy Ginzel

Contributing Proofreaders: Julie Cahalan, Sue Fetters, Nancy Ruhling

Contributing Indexer: Stephanie Reymann, Indexing Solutions

Meredith® Books

Executive Director, Editorial: Gregory H. Kayko

Executive Director, Design: Matt Strelecki

Managing Editor: Amy Tincher-Durik

Executive Editor/Group Manager: Benjamin W. Allen

Senior Associate Design Director: Tom Wegner

Marketing Product Manager: Brent Wiersma

National Marketing Manager—Home Depot: Suzy Johnson

Publisher and Editor in Chief: James D. Blume

Editorial Director: Linda Raglan Cunningham

Executive Director, New Business Development: Todd M. Davis

Director, Sales—Home Depot: Robb Morris

Executive Director, Sales: Ken Zagor

Director, Operations: George A. Susral

Director, Production: Douglas M. Johnston

Director, Marketing: Amy Nichols

Business Director: Jim Leonard

Vice President and General Manager: Douglas J. Guendel

Meredith Publishing Group

President: Jack Griffin

Executive Vice President: Karla Jeffries

Meredith Corporation

Chairman of the Board: William T. Kerr

President and Chief Executive Officer: Stephen M. Lacy

In Memoriam: E.T. Meredith III (1933–2003)

The Home Depot®

Marketing Manager: Tom Sattler

© Copyright 2006 by Homer TLC, Inc.

Some photography © 2006 Meredith Corporation.

First Edition.

All rights reserved.

Printed in the United States of America.

Library of Congress Control Number: 2006932664

ISBN: 978-0-696-23246-6

The Home Depot® is a registered trademark of Homer TLC, Inc.

Distributed by Meredith Corporation.

Meredith Corporation is not affiliated with The Home Depot®.

Note to the Reader: Due to differing conditions, tools and individual skills, Meredith Corporation and The Home Depot® assume no responsibility for any damages, injuries suffered, or losses incurred as a result of attempting to replicate any of the home improvement ideas portrayed or otherwise following any of the information published in this book. Before beginning any project, including any home improvement project, review the instructions carefully and thoroughly to ensure that you or your contractor, if applicable, can properly complete the project, and, if any doubts or questions remain, consult local experts or authorities. Because codes and regulations vary greatly, you should always check with authorities to ensure that your project complies with all applicable local codes and regulations. Always read and observe all of the safety precautions provided by any tool or equipment manufacturer, and follow all accepted safety procedures.

We are dedicated to providing inspiring, accurate and helpful do-it-yourself information. We welcome your comments about improving this book and ideas for other books we might offer to home improvement enthusiasts.

Contact us by any of these methods:

Leave a voice message at: 800/678-2093

Write to:

Meredith Books, Home Depot Books
1716 Locust St.
Des Moines, IA 50309-3023

Send e-mail to: hi123@mdp.com

contents

how to use this book

Building a patio is an investment in the equity of your home and your quality of life as well as a reflection of your style and taste. Remodeling and updating a patio or building a new one can be one of the largest single investments that you will make. The first step in making your dream patio a reality is finding a source of inspiration.

That's why the designers and associates at The Home Depot® have put together a collection of attractive and functional patio designs in one easy-to-use book. *Patios Designs for Living* will inspire you with hundreds of photos and ideas to create an ideal patio for your home and your lifestyle.

Whether you intend to design all or part of the patio yourself or plan to use the services of an architect or designer, you'll need a resource for ideas and some good advice on the latest possibilities for patio designs and styles.

STYLE–FUNCTION–DETAILS. A patio layout that works as well as you need it to is more than a landscape plan and an order for materials; it's a comprehensive design that will turn your dream into reality. A good patio concept is a combination of style, function, and details. It's the result of defining your personal style and taste, considering how you and your family want to use the patio now and in the future, and remembering the finishing touches that will make the space complete.

Style. The style of your patio is a top priority. A design scheme can begin with a specific color, texture, or theme. With the style in place, decisions about paving, furnishings, landscaping, and amenities will be easier. How much time and effort you put into this phase likely will define how happy you'll be using your new patio.

Function. Style is important, but your patio will be underused if its attributes aren't functional. Consider each aspect of your patio—its size, shape, location, materials, and amenities—and whether each aids or hinders the function and enjoyment of your patio. Remember to consider the desires of each family member in your patio design.

Details. To get exactly what you want, plan the finishing touches. The style, colors, and finishes of each element in the patio contribute to a pleasing result. Things you might consider minor—textures and accents for example—will finish the patio in style. It's the purposeful combination of these elements that creates an outdoor room that's unified—and uniquely yours.

ideas

Perhaps no other outdoor structure comes in as many forms as a patio. From a simple slab to a modern, multitier installation, patios expand your living space to the outdoors and add a relaxed dimension to your lifestyle. The following pages take you on a tour of outstanding patio sites, with features and facilities you may be inspired to include in your own backyard retreat.

FALLING WATER

(LEFT) Water spills from the spa, over a ledge of boulders, and into the swimming pool below the patio.

backyard retreats

WHAT YOU MAKE OF IT. There's no one-size-fits-all plan for a patio, no preapproved prescription. Some lifestyles and landscapes work well with a single patio surface, a few pieces of furniture, a grill, and containers full of flowers. Other outdoor living spaces, such as the one featured here, include multiple levels, a pool and spa, a trickling waterfall, an outdoor kitchen, large open areas for entertaining, and a fire pit.

COMMON THREAD. Whatever the style, whatever the conveniences, patios have one thing in common: They provide a place where families can retreat from the pressures of the working world and enjoy a slice of the outdoors. With a patio indulging in an outdoor retreat is simply a matter of stepping out the back door.

DISTINCT SEATING This large backyard is divided into separate spaces, for cooking, eating, conversing, and lounging, all shaded by river birch trees.

OUTDOOR FLOOR Much as flooring indoors provides continuity between rooms, a surface made from rectangular slabs of red-tinged limestone unifies the different functional areas of the patio.

defining spaces

Until it is defined by a boundary, an outdoor space might seem empty and exposed. Patios need containment, a defining edge where they begin and the yard leaves off.

Along the outskirts of your yard, a fence can provide a suitable definition. Close to the house you might need walls, a border of rocks, or planting beds. Defining the outside edges of a patio, however, is insufficient. A successful patio provides clues about the purpose of its inside spaces. Furniture will do that—dining furniture states that the purpose of its space is different from that of the area with lounge chairs. Such furniture groupings create imaginary walls. Subtle structures also can separate patio spaces. Change the pattern in the paving, use a second paving material, or install a low planter to define areas within a large patio.

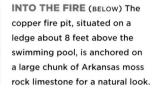

INTO THE FIRE (BELOW) The copper fire pit, situated on a ledge about 8 feet above the swimming pool, is anchored on a large chunk of Arkansas moss rock limestone for a natural look.

PRO PREPPING
(LEFT) This complete kitchen setup features stainless-steel elements including a gas grill, a sink, and undercounter storage that hides a portable water heater.

ELEGANT COMPROMISE Dining space needed to be close to both the kitchen and the outdoor grill. Impossible. The resolution? With the table midway between them, the cook can serve family easily and entertain guests who use the ledges to rest plates and drinks.

INSPIRED IDEAS. Inspiration for outdoor living spaces is endless: A favorite vacation spot, a quiet neighborhood cafe, or a memorable photograph may spark an idea for a patio that seems worlds away. Often all it takes are a few carefully selected elements to set the tone for the entire space. Here cast-iron details and light gray flagstone paving combine to conjure images of an idyllic European setting.

FRAGRANT ESCAPES. Indoor comfort and outdoor beauty—the best patios combine both worlds. Where else can families easily relax and take in the view of fresh flowers and plants? Besides adding visual interest and color, flowers also provide a soft scent that enhances the enjoyment of the space. Fragrant flowers and creeping thyme lend a romantic air to this patio. Whether they're in terra-cotta containers or incorporated into the landscape, lush plantings are one more reason patios are so inviting.

LOUNGING AROUND (ABOVE) Four ample lounge chairs can handle the family traffic to and from the spa. Positioning the spa at the far end of the patio provides privacy from other patio activities.

INTIMATE SPOT (BELOW) Only a few steps from the lounging and dining areas, a quiet niche tucked between the terraces features a domed arbor over a comfortable bench. Stepping-stones lead from the patio to the sitting area—creating a perfect way to escape from the action.

TAKE YOUR PICK

(LEFT) Relaxing by the pool brings a choice of chairs or lounges from the same style line, keeping this space looking unified. So does the running bond brick pattern that ties this area to the outdoor kitchen (opposite).

AWAY FROM IT ALL (BELOW) The dining furniture is similar to the poolside furnishings. It's also light enough to be moved to open up space. Flagstone picks up the character of the fireplace and is more appropriate here than it would be close to the brick house.

GATHERING SPOTS. Comfort ranks high on the list of patio necessities. Family and friends tend to gravitate toward cozy chairs to chat and enjoy the patio's relaxing atmosphere. This patio has multiple clusters of chairs and tables, each reflecting the mood of the individual spaces. Near the house the white dining set and wicker furniture provide spots for taking it easy after a hearty meal. Closer to the backyard the furniture near the pool and stone fireplace takes on an earthy tone.

FLEXIBLE LIVING. Patios are virtual chameleons when it comes to creating different kinds of retreats. On one occasion a section of the patio and a single table can create the perfect mood for a casual dinner party of close friends. On another day the space can accommodate a large family gathering. The lightweight patio furniture is easily moved to open up the space if necessary.

FORMAL ATTIRE

(ABOVE) The wrought-iron table and chairs are not strictly formal in design, but they give this dining space a look fit for formal gatherings. The umbrella helps define the space.

LETTING DOWN

(RIGHT) Both casual and classic, wicker chairs are, above all, comfortable. Their ample size allows for taking it easy after a hearty meal and pleasant conversation.

UNDER THE ROOF (ABOVE) This substantial outdoor porch area includes classic columns, flowing draperies with custom tiebacks, and all of the style of an indoor space.

TIE IT BACK (RIGHT)
The colors of the custom
tiebacks on the draperies
echo the coral, green,
and cream tones found
throughout the space.

STAY OUTSIDE. Filling your patio with items reminiscent of those found in interior rooms—including comfortable furnishings and decorative elements—is the easiest way to ensure that your retreat beckons year-round. In this space the outdoor style of wicker furnishings is softened with cushions and throw pillows covered in colorful, patterned outdoor fabrics. Other items that pair interior touches with outdoor practicality include a bench upholstered in green weather-resistant fabric, weather-safe floor and table lamps, and a soft outdoor area rug that defines the space with a bold splash of color.

CREATURE COMFORTS. To prevent people from traipsing inside in too-hot or too-cool weather, consider ways to regulate the temperature as you would indoors. To keep breezes circulating, plan for the wiring necessary to add a ceiling fan if your patio includes a roof or substantial overhead structure. If evenings tend to be cool, add a portable heater to the space. Draperies such as the ones that surround this patio work wonders too.

COOL BREEZES (BELOW) A ceiling fan was installed in the painted tongue-and-groove ceiling to keep the space cool. Can lights illuminate the space after dark.

UNDERFOOT Just as it does in indoor spaces, an area rug helps define an outdoor room. This one is treated to stand up to wear, tear, and water.

LET THERE BE LIGHT (LEFT) This table lamp, which is rated for outdoor use, would look as good inside as it does out. If electrical outlets aren't included in a patio plan, battery-operated portable lamps function just as well.

WALL STYLE (RIGHT) Vintage china plates and a wrought-iron mirror adorned with whimsical birds add interest to the large brick wall behind the sofa.

MADE FOR THE OUTDOORS (ABOVE) At first glance this patio retreat doesn't even look like an outdoor space, thanks to patterned upholstery fabrics, outdoor lamps, and the decor on the walls. Yet all of the items are made to withstand the elements.

OUT OF THE WOODS A woodburning fireplace, outdoor grill, and dining space are located toward the rear of the yard where it borders a wooded area. The distant location helps keep smoke out of the house.

OPEN AIR (RIGHT)
With openings where walls could be, this roofed patio structure is truly an outdoor room, bringing the natural world into a space with all the comforts of an interior living room.

NATURAL LANDSCAPE. The beauty of the outdoors creates a peaceful setting. To maximize the area's calming effect, work with the yard's natural features. Maybe a cluster of trees creates a shady area perfect for a pair of lounge chairs, or a sloping hill makes a good spot for a waterfall. Here a fireplace and retaining wall are designed to fit the scale of the hill's slope. A "floor" of pea gravel and a mix of greenery soften the stone. The result: an attractive focal point that looks as if it always has been in the landscape.

PURPOSEFUL PLACE. A patio serves several purposes. Often different functional areas are separated by distinctive materials and styles as much as by location. Set away from the house, this patio's fireplace has a rugged, natural feel that sets the scene for family cookouts, while the covered patio next to the home resembles a sitting room perfect for lounging.

Bringing a touch of indoor design to a patio is a great way to make it inviting. Weather-resistant materials are put to good use in the covered portion of this patio. The wicker furniture and water-resistant cushions create spots for an afternoon nap but are hardy enough to withstand a rainstorm. When pulled shut, the floor-to-ceiling drapes will block out raindrops—proving that patios can be enjoyed rain or shine.

CLOSED CASE (LEFT)
Heavy canvas panels mounted on rings on a ceiling-height rod can be pulled across each opening to block out inclement weather.

PRIVATE DINING

(LEFT) Tucked close to the house, the dining area is screened from nearby neighbors by a substantial privacy fence.

entertaining

ENTERTAINING A NOTION. Planning is everything when you're considering party space for your patio. To help keep your excitement up and the stress down, estimate the largest group you'll frequently entertain. Then plan and build the space around that number.

THE SETUP. Making access to any area of the patio easy ensures that a large party easily overflows into adjoining areas. This patio is designed for flexibility. With a series of smaller functional areas within the larger patio, it allows for intimate conversations and small family dinners, as well as large gatherings that span the entire patio. A living room opens to the raised, covered area; the spacious main patio with multiple conversation areas can be accessed from the study and master bedroom; and the dining room and kitchen open to an outdoor dining and grilling space. Raised planters filled with lush foliage and blooms distract from the privacy fence, creating a colorful and private paradise for easy entertaining.

PLANT TALKS (LEFT) In addition to providing comfortable conversation areas, this patio treats guests to views of cascading beds filled with plantings chosen to thrive in the brutal sun and high altitude of Boulder, Colorado.

SHELTERED LIFE The raised portion of the patio accessed via French doors in the living room is protected by an extension of the roof. Skylights welcome sunshine during the day; outdoor lights brighten the space at night.

ALWAYS IN SEASON The main conversation area is near the wall, opening up the patio for other guests. A four-season gazebo gives everyone a chance to get out of the rain.

WARM UP (LEFT) Fire pits bring warmth and a touch of romance to any area. They extend the use of the patio when nights start to cool. This portable unit can be moved where the heat is needed.

MULTIPLE FEATURES. A patio can incorporate several elements that are both functional and eyecatching—an appealing combination when you plan to entertain guests. This gazebo is an immediate focal point and presents an opportunity to include indoor pieces such as a throw rug. It's also practical: The roof and walls provide shelter from weather throughout the year.

Smaller items also add interest and function. This patio's freestanding fire pit has a distinctive look and can be placed where needed. Plump pillows increase the comfort level of wicker furniture. Their bright colors also are punchy accents for an outdoor area. Large or small, interesting and practical pieces are a smart addition to any patio.

ROUNDUP Bright colors are dynamic, and the red umbrella and complementary colors on the pillows and chair seats set the tone for lively entertaining on this inviting patio.

CONSIDERATE HOST. Outdoor entertaining is a simple way to gather friends and family. With a few considerations beforehand, any party will move smoothly. For example, this patio features a dining area just outside the home's dining room. The location makes it quick and easy to transfer dishware and meals from house to patio. It's also convenient if the gathering starts indoors and guests want to venture out later.

Plan ahead to make sure guests will be comfortable. Built-in benches and more than one dining set on this patio ensure that everyone has a place to sit. The stairways connecting different levels of the patio are well lit, which helps guests safely find their way to the fireplace area when the sun sets.

Keep the weather in mind. If it gets chilly a substantial fireplace like this one can create a cozy spot for guests to warm up. Outdoor heat lamps and chimineas also provide warmth for your party, and their soft light contributes to the ambience of a nighttime gathering.

BE OUR GUEST (ABOVE) An expansive upper patio is accessed through three sets of doors from the formal interior dining room (not shown), allowing large gatherings to move smoothly between the exterior and interior.

LEAD THE WAY (BELOW) A brick stairway connects two major areas of the patio—the upper dining level and the lower fireplace area. The brick also adds a rich tone to the neutral stone walls.

SHELTERED GLOW (BELOW) Only steps down from the large upper patio, this alcove offers a protected niche. The fireplace is flanked by built-in benches that provide ample seats from which to enjoy the warmth.

SEPARATE INTERESTS Separating the patio into two distinct areas provides a large space on the left for children and friends and a smaller area on the right for Mom and Dad.

COZY COVE (LEFT) A small gas fire pit cozies up to the low stone wall that defines the perimeter of the patio. A chaise longue makes this an ideal spot for relaxing.

family fun

HAVE IT ALL. By design patios are recreational. With planning a patio can offer almost as many spaces for activities as does the neighborhood park.

PLAYMATES. For some families an effective patio simply is a comfortable space to relax together. This one fits the bill with added amenities, including two gas fire pits, an outdoor kitchen, and an eyecatching fountain. The patio was designed to be spacious enough for the kids to hang out with friends while Mom and Dad entertain too. Creating distinct areas means everyone has a place.

If your needs are more specific, consider the following for your patio plans: Dining surfaces make good craft centers where children can spread out materials. Smooth paving is the perfect surface for tykes on trikes and also for group games. Incorporate a hopscotch court made from painted and sealed stepping-stones. Install a swing and play structure next to the patio and include a sandbox—you can convert it to additional patio space when the children grow. Whatever elements you include for young children, make sure to locate them in clear view so that you can supervise the children's activities.

WATER ART (ABOVE) An old-world fountain is centered on the patio, offering visual interest for the entire space and dividing the functional areas.

DINNER IS SERVED

(ABOVE) The outdoor kitchen is conveniently located near French doors leading to the indoor kitchen. Task lighting and ample counters for food preparation make this an efficient cooking space.

GATHER ROUND

(ABOVE) The design of the freestanding gas fire pit is reminiscent of a campfire. Comfortable rocking chairs encourage conversation.

AT YOUR SERVICE (LEFT)
The large peninsula at the outdoor kitchen serves as a buffet and bar during parties. For family meals it works as a convenient eating counter.

WELCOME HOME (LEFT) A large
slat-roof pergola provides shelter
for relaxation and dining. The
columns add a vertical element to
offset the horizontal lines of the
pool deck.

INCLUSIVE RETREATS. Factoring
kid-friendly elements into a patio can
be compatible with style and design. In
fact it may open up more possibilities
for creativity. On one side of this patio,
a playhouse overlooks the pool and
spa. Matching a playhouse's exterior to
that of the house creates a quaint and
unified design. When children grow older,
the playhouse may be converted into a
pool house.

Designing with the whole family in
mind also can steer you toward cozy
elements. A swing hanging from a pergola
provides a comfortable spot to catch up
with family members after school or
work. A mix of lounging areas and space
for more energetic activities satisfies
everyone in the family. For example a
pair of chairs and a large umbrella near
this pool create a shaded spot for adults
to keep an eye on kids as they splash in
the water.

WIDE-OPEN SPACES. Open and
spacious patios are ideal for active
families—they give children plenty of
space to run and play, but they also allow
adults to keep everyone in sight.

When it's time to bring the group
together, a feature such as the pergola
shown here fits the bill. It's a natural
gathering area given its height and
proximity to the pool. Come together
as a family for an energizing snack or
dinner—before long the kids will be up
and running again.

SMALL WONDER A playhouse designed to look
like a miniature of the house beckons children to play
when it's too chilly for a swim. Mortared flagstone is
a perfect material for the patio surface around the
pool because its rough texture is slip-resistant.

NATURE MADE The usual synthetic look of spa construction may be artfully concealed with natural stone. This design makes one unit of both spa and pool, allowing water to spill from one to the other.

ENDURING DESIGN
(LEFT) Using the same material throughout the shelter helps make it a focal point that balances the lines of the pool. Teak furnishings will endure years of harsh weather.

SECLUDED MEALS
(RIGHT) A combination
of elements creates a
cozy dining area. Brick
walls, leafy plants, a
tall gate, and a garage
surround the patio and
make it ideal for hosting
an intimate dinner.

dining

PURPOSE AND PAVING. Few occasions
top the enjoyment of a meal prepared
outdoors—unless it's the same meal
shared with family or friends. Outdoor
dining space needs to accommodate two
kinds of activities—cooking and dining.
The size of each area will depend on how
you use it.

This patio's smooth concrete paving
adequately supports a table and chairs
for full-scale dining, but a gravel patio
may cause furniture to wobble
or sink. In the latter case pedestal legs
and runners can prove unsinkable.

FITTING FURNITURE. Choose your
tables and chairs with some forethought.
Square and rectangular styles will fit
nicely in rectangular areas but won't seat
odd numbers comfortably. This patio's
round table is more suited for irregular
areas. It's also easier to add or remove
chairs from a round or oval table. Built-in
tables and freestanding islands are other
options especially for casual dining.

Your dining chairs will be the most
highly traveled furnishings on your patio,
so they must be stylish, strong, and light
enough to be moved easily.

COOL GATHERING (BELOW) A border
wall of evergreens provides privacy
and ample shade, and a large umbrella
protects family and friends from the sun
as they enjoy lunch.

WELCOMING ATMOSPHERE
(ABOVE) The table sits close to the gas-
burning brick fireplace, creating the
perfect spot for a late dinner on a cool
summer night.

ALL IN THE DETAILS. Most patios have a few basic elements such as a table and chairs for the family to gather around. These elements are necessary for an enjoyable outdoor space and are great places to inject character and style. A crimson tablecloth and cushions give this patio's classic dining set a cheerful flair. Colorful sculptures and figurines enhance the patio's festive dining area.

It's easy to add spirit to a patio. Unfolding a bright tablecloth takes mere seconds, but the result can change the look of the entire space. Not happy with how it looks? It's just as easy to trade it for one with a different effect. Small garden sculptures and potted plants may be rearranged on a whim. Placing an interesting planter or pitcher on the table is another effortless way to add personal style—not to mention that it can be a great conversation starter when friends are over for a casual dinner.

PERFECT TOUCH (LEFT) Ample dining space for small gatherings rises right out of its floral surroundings—a creative solution to budget limitations. Container-grown plants bring the colors and greenery onto the concrete slab patio, disguising it and providing a welcome decorative touch.

MENAGERIE (RIGHT) Cast figures made just for this purpose dress up what once was a plain wall. Along with the crackle-paint mirror, they create interesting accents and playful distraction.

CANVAS COMFORT
Sail-shape canvas
shades the sitting
area and keeps it cool.
Because they are
small and sectional,
the shades work over
odd-shape areas where
an awning or umbrella
won't do.

IN NO TIME (ABOVE)
Framed by foxgloves and a fountain, this intimate dining space seems stopped in time within its lush setting. Broken concrete adds a rustic, well-worn look.

IRONWORK (BELOW) Black wrought-iron chairs pick up the black and white color scheme on the exterior of the house. The formality of this space is enhanced by urn-shape ledges for potted plants.

SCALING DOWN. A patio's dining area is usually a central spot for socializing and enjoying hearty meals. But also consider the possibilities of creating a smaller, intimate space for mealtimes. Here a pair of wrought-iron chairs and a small bistro table nestle into a courtyard. The nearby fountain completes the calming effect.

Spaces like this one are ideal for peacefully starting the day with a cup of coffee or sharing tea with a close friend in the afternoon. A smaller dining area is also the perfect spot for a romantic dinner by candlelight.

ENCLOSED SPACES. Open and sprawling or secluded and enclosed, patios vary greatly in design. This patio takes on the character of a European courtyard, complete with broken concrete slabs and tall stucco garden walls. If your space lacks garden walls, place a small dining set close to the house or garage for a similar effect.

END OF IT ALL (ABOVE) A cast medallion and statue of a small boy on a pedestal signal the end of the journey on the stepping-stone path.

choosing the site

You're thinking about installing a patio, which means you probably have ideas about how you want to use it. That's good because patio planning begins with a look at your lifestyle—at what you and your family like to do. Patios are versatile. They can include space for quiet reflection, areas for casual dining, places for play, room for large parties—or all these activities together.

PROTECTED PARADISE Slate tile quietly anchors this dining area on a sheltered patio, bringing an effective contrast to the active colors and textures that surround it.

planning
activities

TWO TO GO (ABOVE) Brick stairs from the kitchen and breezeway offer easy access and help unify this patio with the house. Both cooking and dining spaces are scaled for small group gatherings.

LIFESTYLE LIST. Get the family together and make a list of everything everyone would like to include in your new patio. Think freely and ignore costs—you'll pare the list down later. Making a lifestyle list will help jumpstart your plans.

FIRST THINGS FIRST. Next prioritize the list. If you'll use the patio for intimate dining but want to entertain now and then, you can design the space to handle the occasional crowd without altering the ambience for quiet meals.

Then study the terrain of your yard, the treelines, traffic patterns, and any hardscapes. They can affect your plans. So can views and climate. A slope might suggest a tiered patio. A constantly sunny spot might benefit from a covered structure. And prevailing winds call for windscreens. Then there's rainwater: Be sure that moisture moves off the surface and away from the house.

DRAINED OUT

(BELOW) Patio surfaces should be gently pitched to keep rainwater from puddling on them. Large patios may require an internal drain to keep their paving dry.

objects and obstacles

Existing elements in your landscape, such as trees, large rocks, and planting beds, may have acquired permanent status and seem like obstacles to your planning. Use them instead of moving them or losing them. Treat them as opportunities, not problems.

Whenever possible, make permanent landscape features part of your design. Trees can become the perfect focal point for a patio, bring shade, and add a vertical complement to a patio's strong horizontal plane. Boulders and large rocks worked into the perimeter can stop patio space from spilling into other areas of the yard, making your outdoor room feel cozy and integrating it into its natural surroundings.

ON STAGE Although the umbrella shades the space in the absence of trees, it also helps make this patio the focal point of the landscape. Contrasting materials set the tone for both quiet dining and entertainment.

WATER WAYS (ABOVE) What could fit more naturally in a patio setting than a relaxing waterfall, pond, and plants? Modern materials make building a water feature easier than it may look.

SERENE SPOT (RIGHT) Tucked amid a surround of blooms and lacy-foliage shrubs and trees, this hideaway enjoys the right amount of privacy for intimate gatherings.

MAKING A CONNECTION (RIGHT) Pathways of mixed limestone and loose rock link separate patio areas—a good way to take advantage of a long yard.

location

PLACEMENT PLANNING. Patios traditionally are located at the rear of the house because backyards typically provide a measure of privacy. But you can situate your patio almost anywhere. Front-yard patios might make the entrance to your home more welcoming. A side-yard patio can turn otherwise wasted lawn space into a room for outdoor living.

SITING SOLUTIONS. Most patios are situated close to the house. If outdoor dining figures in your plans, you'll want your patio within easy reach of the kitchen. A detached patio sheltered by trees or shrubs offers a pleasant spot for solitude and contemplation.

Look to the shape of your house for clues to patio location. Courtyard patios tucked into inside corners of the house come with ready-made privacy. A wraparound patio provides a solution for families who want an outdoor room for entertaining as well as space for solitude.

SCREEN TEST (ABOVE)
Many sites will require some alteration to make them the perfect patio spot. This backyard location needed the pergola and latticework to screen out the neighboring garage.

BACKBEAT (RIGHT)
A remote patio tied to the rest of the yard by a stepping-stone path provides a secluded retreat at the back of this landscape.

take in **the view**

A pleasant view puts the finishing touch on patio design. If you're lucky to glimpse a mountain or a cityscape, orient your patio to take in the view. If such stunning vistas are not available, you still can find—or make—enticing scenes.

Walk around your prospective patio site and look for interesting details outside its perimeter. Maybe it's the treeline in the neighbor's yard or the shapes of nearby buildings. Often you can make uneventful sights interesting by framing them with tall shrubs or with the selective placement of screens. A glimpse of an otherwise mundane object can prove inviting to the eye. If the views to the outside prove less than enticing, careful arrangement of colorful planting beds or potted foliage can create a visual treat surrounding your patio.

SUNKEN TREASURE (BELOW) Groundcover holds back the slope on this patio, and potted ferns, spreading branches, and a slatted fence combine to create a hideaway just out the back door.

TAKE TWO (LEFT)
Multiple patios make the most of sloped lots and walkout lower levels. This lower patio offers a quiet respite for two while the upper offers views for a gathering.

OVER SITE (ABOVE) With the right foundation, rooftops can provide great locations for patios. Tempered-glass panels keep the view open and safe for the kids. Color contrasts and furnishings set the style and separate the spaces according to purpose.

SIDE WALK (RIGHT)
A brick walkway makes use of the otherwise obstructive curve of the window well as it moves toward the stone benches at the rear of this tranquil setting.

OUT LOUNGING
(ABOVE) French doors with coordinating sidelights open the view from the inside of the house to the patio. Even a smaller patio benefits from easy and inviting access.

access

AN OPEN INVITATION. Access to your patio from the interior of your home—both physical and visual—contributes to whether the patio invites you outside and becomes integral to your lifestyle.

EASY DOES IT. Access should be easy. Multiple doors are ideal especially for party guests passing to and from the patio. Double doors, such as French doors, or atrium or sliding doors provide good visual and physical access. The expanse of glass diminishes the perceived separation between the indoors and outdoors. Use the same flooring materials for both the interior room and patio to heighten the continuity between spaces.

Provide a clear path to the patio, rearranging the furniture in the adjacent room if necessary. And plan so that you don't have to step down to the patio by more than a few inches.

LOOK OUT (ABOVE) Large doors and wide windows open the interior room to the patio, making both spaces seem like extensions of each other and facilitating the free flow of family and guests.

FLIGHT OF FANCY

(LEFT) Stairways provide access but should be more than simply functional. Here white blossoms carry the color down the steps, blending the Civil War-era metalwork into the design while celebrating its uniqueness.

CLOSE AT HAND (BELOW) Placing the dining table near the kitchen entrance and the lounge chairs close to the breezeway door maximizes the convenience of getting to this patio.

LANDING ZONES (ABOVE) Building outdoor steps deeper than indoor steps and adding landings make climbing slopes easier. Here ashlar bluestone walls stylishly hold back the soil.

SAFETY FEATURES
(LEFT) Textures make steps slip-resistant, lighting illuminates the way, and handrails often are required by code. Most safety features can be integrated by using complementary colors.

interior rooms

What goes on in the interior room adjacent to the patio can impact how often you use the patio.

Plan your patio so it's as close as possible to an interior room with activities that closely match the patio space. For example, patio dining or cooking is best located close to the kitchen. An entertainment area works near a family room or dining room but not outside the master bedroom. Build a separate patio outside the bedroom to reserve a spot for morning coffee. If the patio doubles as play space, locate it outside the family room and make sure you have a clear line of sight to supervise activities.

size

PURPOSE AND SCALE. A patio for intimate dining requires little space. For entertaining you'll need room for a crowd. Building the right size patio also depends on the scale of your house. A 10 × 10-foot area will handle two chairs and a small table. But attach it to a large house and it will look too small. If you're designing space for a single person, make one dimension at least 6 feet. For a family patio start with a 10 × 20-foot area.

SPACING THINGS OFF. Allow space for each outdoor furnishing plus a comfort zone around it and passage to and from it. Always sketch a plan for furnishings on graph paper. Factor in the size of any structures such as low walls or planters.

A SEPARATE PEACE (ABOVE) Although the size of the pool is modest, the sculpted deck is large enough to accommodate an area for intimate conversation as well as shaded poolside dining.

SIDE WISE (RIGHT) Adding a grill and accessories turns this side yard into a cozy dining space. Container plantings and a sweep of branches overhead increase its intimacy.

CATERED COMFORT

(ABOVE) Detached or remote patios might mean catering your own brunch or dinner, but a small patio area at the end of a path like this makes good use of open terrain without overpowering the garden elements.

A NARROW INTERPRETATION

(RIGHT) Making use of narrow space can require creative furniture arrangement. With plenty of access behind them, the chairs and table sit at an angle to allow traffic to move easily around them.

CAST IN STONE Cut-stone paving and limestone repeated in the walls and fireplace help unify several patio areas in this large space. Planting beds and container gardens soften the texture of the stone.

sizing it up

Many otherwise well-planned patios end up being too small, so if anything err on the side of making yours too large. Start with the recommendations below and set furnishings on the lawn for a trial run. Expand the space if any area feels even the slightest bit cramped.

▶ **DINING AREAS** for four take up about 10 × 10 feet. For six to eight people, make it 12 × 12 feet.

▶ **ROUND TABLES** with six chairs require space with a diameter of at least 9 feet.

▶ **RECTANGULAR TABLES** fit best in an area 5 to 6 feet larger on all sides.

▶ **GRILLS WITH SMALL TABLES** take up an area about 6 feet square—add more for a counter or island.

▶ **PASSAGE** from the door to the stairs and between activity areas should be at least 3½ to 4 feet wide at all points.

IN THE LONG RUN
Emphasizing the length of this space, especially by placing a separate seating area at a distance, leads the eye outward, shifting attention from how confined the space is.

FLOOR SPACE (ABOVE) A compact worktable provides prep space next to a hefty grill. The dining table is positioned close to the grill yet out of traffic moving between the patio and house.

EAT OUT (BELOW) A two-tone pebbled-concrete pad offers enough room for an elegant alfresco dining area. The oval table comfortably seats eight while nestling into the tight space.

small-space solutions

MINOR WONDERS. A diminutive yard can make the perfect spot for an outdoor room. Small patios have to work carefully to avoid feeling cramped, but they let you create cozy and secluded places. Two design principles work wonders in small spaces—simplicity and use of elements that make the space look larger than it is.

FOOLING THE EYE. Alter the perception of size by using glazed doors so the outdoors seems to extend into the interior. Draw attention to the space around the patio with lines and patterns that lead the eye outward. Blurring the borders of the patio with curved planting beds softens its edges. Increase the usable area by opening its center and placing furnishings strategically along the sides. Built-in seating takes up less room than freestanding pieces, and the right mix of both will add flexibility to a small area.

UPSHOT Vertical lines, such as those of this fireplace, the chimney, the tall window sections, and high doorways, keep the eye moving away from the confines of a small patio area.

COLORFUL CHARACTERS (LEFT)
Repainting old lawn furniture and placing a few colorful plants around the patio create an outdoor composition that seems larger than it is.

NO ACCIDENT
(ABOVE) In small spaces everything gets intense scrutiny. Here the artful placement of the paving stones results from meticulous planning, not happenstance.

A MATTER OF SCALE (LEFT)
This family-size outdoor room seems to begin at the back door and flow into the lawn. Curved lines look less confining than straight ones, and the child's picnic table adds a whimsical accent in exactly the right scale.

...hese
...ep
...ir
...style.
...s into the
perimeter planting beds.

STAGES (BELOW)
Covered porchways
add an intermediate
transition between
the house and
patio. Large party
areas are enhanced
by multiple doors,
allowing guests
to move in and
out easily.

transitions

BRIDGES. Smooth transitions can unite indoor and outdoor spaces. They help signify that your living space doesn't end inside the door but extends into the outdoors too. Those transitions, however, represent only a fraction of what patios can do to bridge spaces in a landscape.

Patios can serve as passages between your house and other outdoor areas such as a public parkway, lush gardens, a swimming pool, or a nearby beach.

TRANSITIONAL TOOLBOX. Patios designed to connect long sections of a landscape or slopes provide a unique opportunity to add outdoor rooms with different purposes. Experiment with materials and textures to create stunning visual effects while defining that each area is meant for a specific function. Pave a spot for family dining close to the house with smooth slate. Then set the next level for entertaining with brick or cut stone in a sand bed. Stairs, steps, and paths add to your palette of transitional tools. Be sure to include some consistent materials and colors from space to space to avoid a disjointed effect.

NATURALLY (ABOVE) Large limestone slabs, embellished with potted blooming plants, arc their way comfortably from one level to another. Natural stone imparts an informal look, one that seems to grow right out of the landscape.

ON THE RISE (ABOVE)
Different levels double the interest of this patio space and the surrounding gardens. Removing soil from one area and using it to elevate another creates tiers on level terrain.

ROCKY ROAD (RIGHT)
Exposed aggregate makes an inexpensive, stylish material for walkways. Spaces that lack interest may be touched up with decorative accents like these rustic chairs.

SIDE TRIP (LEFT) A Victorian side entrance is enhanced by a brick walk from the street. In front the paving matches the formality of the porch, but a change of pattern signals a journey to more casual areas back of the house.

FORMAL INVITATION (BELOW) The formality of a brick "doorway" and fanned steps create a definite boundary where the lawn ends and the patio begins.

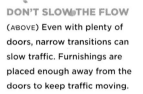

DON'T SLOW THE FLOW
(ABOVE) Even with plenty of doors, narrow transitions can slow traffic. Furnishings are placed enough away from the doors to keep traffic moving.

LOOKING GLASS (ABOVE)
A narrow porch provides a stately transition to outdoor dining and a spa. Tempered-glass panels keep the narrow passage from feeling confined.

SEEMINGLY SEAMLESS
(BELOW) Wide doors ease the transition from inside out. An ample roof overhang provides a stopping spot so eyes can adjust to the outdoor light.

path principles

Paths simply can move you from one place to another or make an enticing design statement through the use of a few uncomplicated principles.

First be sure the design of your path matches its purpose. Then, where possible, add interest along its journey. If its job is to get you from the potting shed to the planting bed, a straight walk will do. But a path meandering along the yard in curves between patio sections feels enticing, mysterious, and full of surprises, especially if at the end of a curve you come upon a covered bench, a trickling fountain, or a waterfall. Even a sculptural accent creates a delightful surprise. A successful path is one that takes you somewhere—to an area for family play, a garden reserved for herbs, or even back to its beginning.

EASY DOES IT The cut-stone patio and running bond brick walkway mirror architectural elements of the house in color and form. Such unifiers help bring the house out into the landscape and garden areas, blending elements seamlessly.

TEA FOR THREE (LEFT) Trees with delicate foliage and open latticework panels help keep this cozy setting from feeling walled in.

JUST RIGHT (BELOW) Adding the right measure of privacy keeps a patio open and airy. A 6-foot fence works where a taller structure might seem confining.

privacy & enclosure

NOTABLE ABSENCE. Privacy and a sense of enclosure are essential to good patio design. A patio that's completely open will leave you feeling exposed.

VERSATILE SOLUTIONS. Tuck the patio in a corner of the house. Shrubs, hedges, fences, and walls make good privacy screens. Be cautious, however, about creating complete privacy; it can make your patio feel confining. Vine-covered latticework, low fences, and plants with delicate foliage create shelter without hemming you in. They also hide unsightly objects such as air-conditioners and trash containers.

Don't forget to look up. Intimate spots feel cozy with overheads 8 to 10 feet high. Areas for entertaining feel right with tree branches or other ceilings 20 feet above.

DOUBLE DUTY
A gate is a visual and physical cue that the space beyond is private. Yet the low open design of this one still beckons guests.

PRIVACY AT POOL TIME
A pool house with a kitchen and seating areas provides a spot for enjoying the backyard even if the weather isn't right for spending time outdoors. The hues of the structure's materials match those around the pool.

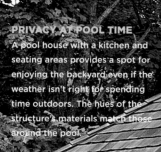

BACKYARD BISTRO (ABOVE)
Existing trees and shrubs can
provide an inexpensive and ready-
made solution to a multitude of
privacy problems.

SPA SOLITUDE

(LEFT) A wooden fence and evergreens offer year-round privacy for the spa. Distance adds to perceived privacy. Positioning the spa on a pad slightly away from the main patio offers a sense of seclusion.

GARDEN ROOM

(LEFT) A vine-covered arbor with lattice frames defines the edges of this outdoor room and provides selective privacy, filtered breezes, and dappled shade.

GREAT ESCAPE

(ABOVE) Every detail of this space—the wall of the shed, the ferns and other plants overhead, and the gated section of fence—contributes to the private ambience of this intimate enclosure.

privacy—**selective and strategic**

Privacy for patios comes in different forms and quantities. It's important to tailor privacy structures to the purpose of the space.

Spaces such as retreats for reading or reflection require more privacy than spaces for public activities such as entertaining. Walls, fences, dense foliage, and arbors with climbing plants can provide sufficient privacy for places of repose. Partial screens such as lattice and plants with delicate foliage will shelter areas for children's play or gatherings. Place structures strategically. For example, find the angle from which you're most exposed and install a section of privacy fence only in that spot. The closer you locate the structure to the patio, the more complete protection it offers.

materials

Choosing materials is the point at which patio planning becomes a creative endeavor. Now that you've accounted for the abstract elements in your design, such as size, shape, and placement, you can get your hands on the materials that will contribute most to the style of your patio and your enjoyment of the space.

choosing materials

BALANCING ACT. Aesthetics, location, and cost are factors when choosing patio paving. In general paving near the house should be complementary to the home's style. The modular forms of brick, tile, cut stone, and pavers make attractive floors, and their flat surfaces keep furniture from wobbling. Flagstone's random shapes may better suit patios partnered with an informal house style. Loose materials offer a soft base for children's activities. Using more than one paving material to visually divide a large patio provides a signal that you're entering space with a different purpose.

Material colors also contribute to the ambience. Light-color paving will brighten a shaded spot. Sunny spaces feel cooler with nonreflective surfaces.

PAVING PERSONALITIES. Paving materials behave differently and not all are equally suited to all purposes. Some are frostproof. Others are slip-resistant. Some store heat; others reflect it. Consider all the characteristics of a material and pick the paving that best fits both purpose and climate.

STRONG LINES
(ABOVE) The linear
quality of this
brick patio and
fireplace is broken
up by the gentle
curves of the
seating along the
hearth area.

DISCREET PRIVACY
(LEFT) Raised planters
filled with lush flowers and
bushes distract from the
stucoo-color wood fence
that surrounds this stone-
paved patio.

IN SCALE (RIGHT)
Stone is available in larger sizes than other materials, making it ideal for the scale of large outdoor structures such as this fireplace.

stone

PERFECTLY NATURAL. Stone lends a natural character to a patio. Its medley of colors, surfaces, and shapes makes it an ideal fit for any style. Choose a variety local to your region to reduce costs.

QUALITIES. Sandstones and limestones, perhaps the most common patio stones, come in colors ranging from dark reds to off-whites. Their densities vary, and some—such as travertine, whose pitted surfaces can be smoothed with synthetic fillers—require sealing to ward off stains.

Bluestone is a strong stone that resists cracking. Its colors, primarily a subtle array of blues and greens, won't fade.

Slates—some as soft as marble, others as hard as granite, most with a slightly ridged surface—make a naturally slip-resistant patio floor. Slate occurs in a number of greens, grays, and blues.

Granite is a tough, multicolor stone that stands up to freezing, stains, and heavy use.

Quartzite is exceptionally hard and exhibits the best qualities of stone. It's nonporous, easy to clean, and its neutral colors won't fade.

PATTERN OF EXCELLENCE

(ABOVE) Natural stone makes the perfect edging for water features, and its varied forms create endless pattern possibilities.

STEPPING-STONES (LEFT)

Pebble finishes are durable and both algae- and slip-resistant, making them an excellent material choice in installations where safety is critical.

LONG DIVISION Mortared limestone makes attractive low border walls, especially when its hard edges are softened by carefully chosen greenery.

FRIEZE FRAME (ABOVE) A section of salvaged friezework makes a pleasant accent with the groundcover on this stone path.

OUTDOOR FLOOR (ABOVE) The neutral hues of these stone tiles provide a connection to the outdoors, while the arrangement of the tiles mimics that of tile flooring found inside the home.

GREEN SPACE (BELOW) Flagstone lends itself to many design possibilities. Joints can be sanded or mortared, and strategic plantings, as on this patio, can make the floor of the space look natural.

on the surface

The popularity of patios has expanded design possibilities for patio stone.

▸ **FLAGSTONE** is cut or cleft (split) into irregular slabs from 1 to 2 inches thick and 1 to 4 feet wide.

▸ **CUT STONE** is sawn into flat squares and rectangles from 4 to 20 inches wide.

▸ **STONE TILE** and **STONE VENEER** are cut stone $3/4$-inch or less thick.

▸ **COBBLESTONES** are handhewn into cubes, rectangles, or cylinders.

▸ **RIVER ROCK** is any stone variety rounded by the forces of glaciers or water.

LOOK-ALIKE (ABOVE) Pool decks should be wide, safe, and attractive. Colored and stamped concrete offers an inexpensive option that meets requirements for safety and is low-maintenance.

BUDGET CUT (ABOVE) Random but well-planned cuts in a newly poured concrete slab impart an interesting, modern pattern to this affordable paving material.

A NATURAL LOOK (ABOVE) The colorful swirls of these stained concrete squares help them blend with the surrounding plantings, potted plants, and chiminea.

concrete

STEP ON IT (BELOW) A pebbly stone-face concrete pad creates visual interest and texture on a brand-new patio.

SALON DE CONCRETE. Coloring and stamping are the beauty secrets of concrete. A versatile paving material, concrete doesn't have to suffer its natural gray. Give it the look of brick or flagstone for less cost than the real thing.

FANCY FINISHES. Techniques can be used by themselves or in conjunction with other finishes to dress up concrete. Fine aggregate embedded in the surface creates a modestly colorful and slip-resistant surface. Rock salt produces a pock-marked patina that resembles travertine. And simply adding a colorant can enhance its looks dramatically. If you inherited a drab slab, stain it with dyes or resurface it with a new layer of concrete.

BRICK BLEND Brick in various forms presents itself in this outdoor space. The antiqued stucco planters are faced with red brick, while the floors are formed brick for a more rustic appearance.

brick

STANDING ON CHARACTER.
Brick lends stately character to a patio. You'll find an array of colors—with shades ranging from burgundies to whites—and styles. Make sure the color and texture suit the architecture of your home. Stay away from common brick, face brick, and firebrick—they're not designed for paving. Purchase brick rated for your climate.

PATTERN PLANNING.
Identify the most attractive pattern for your setting. Simple patterns will reduce installation costs, while complex designs such as herringbone can create stunning effects. Most brick patios tend toward the formal, but salvaged brick gives a charming casual look.

FULL OF FORMALITY (ABOVE) The classic formal nature of brick makes it the ideal paving material for this lavish formal patio. The ruddy brown tones of the brick are offset by the crisp white of the overhead structure, the trimwork on the house, and the furnishings.

POINTS OF DEPARTURE (BELOW) Brick lends itself to unusual outlines, especially when combined with active patterns such as this herringbone design. It also creates a safe surface near water and requires minimal upkeep.

BLOCKED IN (BELOW) Cut into the brick walk at periodic intervals, splashes of alternate material such as these granite blocks make an interesting accent.

MEDALLIONS (RIGHT) As an example of the versatility of tile, glazed pieces set in cut tile squares and in the brick itself spice up this rustic basket weave pattern.

PAVING IN PORCELAIN (BELOW) Porcelain pavers have become an increasingly popular patio material. They're hard, virtually waterproof and maintenance-free, and their colors will match any theme, such as this creamy off-white that blends with the stone walls and the stairs.

TILED IN STYLE (ABOVE) Terra-cotta or other slip-resistant tile makes a good paving choice for pool surrounds. Color is important too. Here the red tile provides a pleasant complement to the blue tones sprinkled throughout the design.

EARTHTONES Tans and earthtones in this mosaic spa enclosure help blend it into its outdoor surroundings.

ceramic tile

THE HARD FACTS. Select a tile rated for your climate because not all tiles will stand up to freezes. Porcelain tile—a hard, vitreous ceramic—is suitable for winter climates and comes in a variety of sizes and colors. Many resemble moderately textured stone. Quarry tile is fired at high temperatures, making it a material suitable for most climates. Cement-bodied tile is a mortar-and-sand material that is cured, not fired. Mesh-backed cement-bodied sheets can mimic the look of cleft stone at a lower price. Terra-cotta tile isn't really ceramic because it's fired at low temperatures, but it's suitable for climates that stay above freezing.

RUNNING IN CIRCLES (RIGHT) Precast pavers can create a variety of geometric patterns. Swirls such as these give the paving a visual intensity, and the individual sections help mark different patio usage areas.

CHECKMATE (ABOVE) A checkerboard pattern of pavers in two gray hues adds visual interest to a small, square patio.

cement-bodied pavers

A CONCRETE EXAMPLE. Pavers are made from pressure-cast concrete shaped to look like brick or stone. Their low cost and array of sizes, colors, and shapes account for their increasing popularity.

PAVING THE WAY. Cement-bodied pavers fall into two categories: standard rectangular or square pavers and interlocking pavers with contoured shapes that keep them in place. Colors stay in the warm hues, with reds, browns, and earthtones. All are intended for a sand-bed installation. Most come with spacing tabs molded on the edges. A variety of textures—from smooth to aggregate—adds to their style.

STONE SOLUTION (LEFT) The stones used along the edge of this pond to disguise the liner also top a stone wall on the opposite side of the water feature.

FAIR GAME (ABOVE) Cedar chips become the comfortable floor of this outdoor game room and provide contrasting "grout" lines for the rough stepping-stone path. The top of the wooden bench has a painted checkerboard to while away the time.

TREAD SOFTLY
(RIGHT) Pea gravel makes for comfortable walking even in bare feet. Its quiet crunching underfoot adds a soothing sound to this formal layout.

loose materials

ON THE LOOSE (BELOW) This rock does more than separate the flagstones in the path. It adds a visual contrast that makes the path continuously interesting.

LOOSELY SPEAKING. The realm of patio paving extends beyond hard, modular products. Loose materials change the textural character of a patio, lower its cost, and improve drainage.

A ROUGH IDEA. Consider compacted surface properties and how the materials feel underfoot. Decomposed granite and lava rock generally compact into a firm surface that migrates little. They're rough on bare feet though. Pea gravel is more comfortable. River rock brings fascinating textures to a patio. On traveled areas keep its size under 2 inches and as consistent as possible. Shredded bark and wood chips are softest, but they require more replenishing and tend to stray from their appointed area.

SLATED FOR SUCCESS (ABOVE)
Slate tiles intermixed with river rock
and anchored in a concrete bed make
an attractive and maintenance-free
walkway.

TRUE BLUE (ABOVE)
This path meandering
through a stone-tile patio
features bluestone rubble
embedded in concrete.
Color contrasts such
as this provide a
pleasant surprise.

mixing
materials

CARNIVAL OF CONTRASTS. The
careful employment of contrasting colors,
shapes, sizes, and textures is central to
good design. A hardscape mosaic that
mixes materials can solve tricky issues.

Use loose materials with hardscape,
limestone edging with river rock. Let
grass grout a stepping-stone path or
create a collage with brick, cut stone,
and slate. Save money by using local
sandstone and setting brick between
the stone slabs; combine river rock with
pavers for a multitextured space. Let
the contrasts take precedence—sharply
defined boundaries between materials
are rarely needed.

EASING UP A spread of rubble rock between the lawn and pool edging adds an easygoing transition to this pool. The rubble, along with the plantings, eases the hard edges of the large stones and softens their impact in the landscape.

OVERVIEW (ABOVE) Large boulders strewn along the stream, ashlar limestone ringing the walls, and the cut-stone cap all work together to create a naturalistic patio setting in an urban environment.

PERFECT PERCH (BELOW) Built-in wood benches on stone foundations provide sturdy, permanent seating for an outdoor "living room." The wood draws out the warm brown tones in the stones.

go
ma

Some regula others attention. Factor in maintenance during material selection because inexpensive materials may cost more in the long run.

Soft sandstones are porous and likely to stain. This may be a minor problem for a detached woodland retreat, but repeated exposure to food stains in an outdoor dining area may mean frequent scrubbing or periodic sealing. Loose materials will need replenishing now and then, but a tight sand-bed paving probably requires only minor sweeping and fresh sand occasionally. With an annual sweeping or hosing, a mortared patio can last a lifetime.

Design your patio as a low- or no-maintenance living space from the outset. That way you'll spend your time enjoying the space instead of repairing it.

RIGHT MIX (LEFT) Distinctive patio areas often are distinguished by different materials. Here buff-color pavers around the pool give way to a rustic brick staircase.

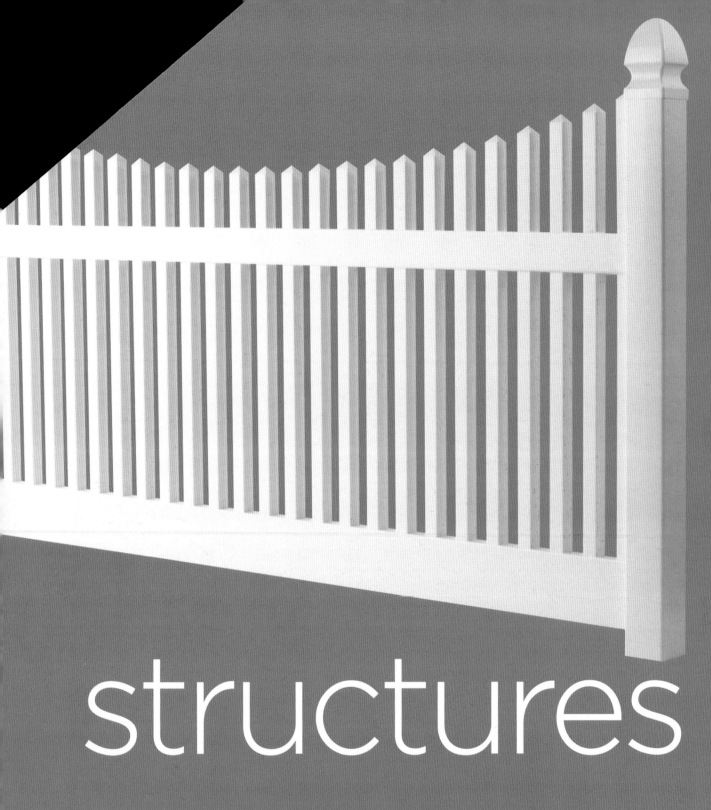

structures

Whatever else your patio is, ornate or modest, fully equipped or quietly functional, you'll want it to be comfortable—not too hot, not too cool, soothed by soft breezes, and a haven from harsh weather and insects. Making a patio enjoyable means planning for comfort right from the start.

FILTERS (ABOVE) Closely spaced pergola rafters and a slatted fence filter harsh sunlight and strong winds, keeping this patio comfortable with dappled shade and gentle breezes.

UPON REFLECTION
(LEFT) This oversize umbrella casts shade beyond the edges of the table and its white fabric reflects the sun's heat up and away from it.

planning for comfort

LUXURIOUS ZONES. The best way to plan for comfort is to think about how you plan to use your patio and how microclimates throughout your yard might influence those activities.

Where you put your patio affects its temperature. In general northern exposures get the least amount of light and may prove too cool. Sunlight warms a southern exposure most of the day. East-facing patios will be warm in the morning but probably too cool for an evening meal. West-facing patios experience the reverse.

Sun, shade, and wind patterns vary from yard to yard. Study your landscape to make the best use of nature's heating and cooling. If natural shade is absent, make your own with a pergola, umbrella, or awning. For extended comfort consider a gazebo or other roofed structure.

HOLDING UP (RIGHT)
Large pillars, beams, and rafters seem to support the mass of tree branches overhead, framing the entrance to the poolside dining space.

overhead structures

THINGS ARE LOOKING UP. Overhead structures such as arbors and pergolas do more than create enclosure and add vertical interest. They make shade. As a bonus the right design also can transform an average-looking patio into a one-of-a-kind installation.

UNITIES OF FORM. Overheads come in all sizes and shapes and sport any number of ceiling patterns. What matters is that yours integrates itself into your landscape design. Link it to your home by repeating a detail on the house, finishing it in a similar color, or using a common architectural accent.

Study sun exposure before designing the ceiling of your structure. In one location it may need only simple slats to shade a patio; another might call for trelliswork, vines, and climbing plants. Whatever your design your goal is to create filtered, not total, shade, and you'll want that shade crossing your patio during the times you use it. It's OK if your pergola or overhead covers only part of the area. That way you can use part of the site in full sun when you want to.

ENTRANCING ARBOR (BELOW)
This arched arbor mirrors the arc of the branches beyond it, creating a sense of enclosure in the entrance and anticipating the intimacy of the patio space inside.

FASCINATING RHYTHMS Varying the placement of ceiling slats and fence boards and adding curved gussets creates rhythms that make this pergola stylish and functional.

CONNECT IT (ABOVE)
A simple white pergola connects this Arts and Crafts-style home to the nearby outdoor fireplace. The pergola also provides shade for the outdoor kitchen area.

GRAND ENTRANCE (RIGHT)
A Baroque cornice and classic columns make this arbor a stylish focal point. Flowering vines entwined through the lattice create peaceful shade, enhancing the solitude surrounding the ornate bench seat.

ARBOR VIEW (LEFT)
Doubled arches increase the architectural interest of this arbor and offer a sense of enclosure.

OVERHEAD ART (ABOVE)
This unusual metal overhead structure provides more graphic interest than it offers shade. The expansive structure defines an entry-area patio and deck.

DESERT DESIGN

(ABOVE) Handhewn latillas fastened to strong viga rafters provide a grid of shade from an overhead structure that completes this modern Southwestern theme.

NATURAL STYLE (LEFT)

The tightly woven domelike top of this pergola provides a spot for lush vegetation to grow and shades a seating area set away from the house. The natural wood of the canopy fits with the rustic furnishings.

gazebos

BACKYARD BANDSTANDS. A gazebo is
a multifaceted structure. It makes a stylish
shelter from the rain but lets you enjoy the
storm. Build one next to your patio or tuck
it away as a retreat. Use it to shelter diners
or as space for quiet conversation during
large gatherings.

A FITTING ADDITION. The style should
fit your plans for the area. Design the
window frames—open, screened, or with
storm windows—to suit the activities you
plan for the space.

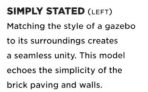

SIMPLY STATED (LEFT)
Matching the style of a gazebo to its surroundings creates a seamless unity. This model echoes the simplicity of the brick paving and walls.

CONVERSATION PIECE (BELOW)
Reminiscent of its Victorian counterparts, this large gazebo creates space for conversation and is accented with flower-filled baskets and containers.

TONY COVER (BELOW) Umbrellas come in an overwhelming selection of styles and colors. This model fits well with the tones in the flagstone patio and the rock face of the pull-up bar area.

awnings & umbrellas

SHADE MAKERS. Any patio site lacking trees or other shade will almost certainly benefit from an awning or umbrella. Retractable awnings are practical for keeping outdoor spaces comfortable. In addition retractable awnings cool the interior of your house in the summer and let sunshine in during the winter. They're especially effective on east and west windows. Umbrellas also are multipurpose additions. Freestanding umbrellas make shade portable. Table umbrellas offer more selective shade. Awnings and umbrellas add privacy by blocking views from higher perspectives such as neighbors' windows.

AT YOUR SERVICE Retractable awnings allow shelter to be tailored to weather conditions. Motor-driven models activated with the touch of a button make adjustments simple.

OVER THE TOP
Canvas draped loosely between ceiling slats puts the finishing touches on this revivalistic shade structure that is part awning, part pergola.

BY DEFINITION

(RIGHT) This umbrella shades an outdoor conversation circle and helps define the space. The umbrella can be moved easily on starlit evenings when there's a fire in the fire pit.

WINGING IT (BELOW) Triangular awning shapes reminiscent of wings bring a futuristic touch to the modern setting below. They shelter the space while still leaving it open to the sky.

IN ITS ELEMENT

(ABOVE) In yards too limited for a detached structure such as a gazebo, a roofed area attached to the house offers shelter.

roofs

MODERATING EXTREMES. In moderate climates the boundaries between indoors and outdoors blur, with one leading smoothly to the other. In other areas, however, a roofed structure can determine whether you enjoy outdoor living space or stay indoors.

FULL OR PARTIAL. Roofed structures such as screened patios can extend your outdoor experience into all seasons. They add a barrier between you and inclement weather and insects. With tinted screens or windows they increase privacy.

You can add smaller, space-specific roofs over outdoor cooking areas to improve the space's functionality with little additional cost. Such partial roofs can provide sheltered space for meals. Their obvious presence requires a style integral to the overall design scheme.

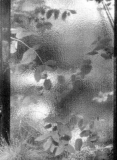

OUT OF THE ZONE
An enclosed greenhouse gives the avid gardener a place to extend the joys of gardening with plants not suited to colder climates. Patterned glass helps make this a private space by obscuring the view.

PATTERN OF CHANGE (RIGHT)
Interrupting the pattern of a wall reduces repetition and increases interest. An inset of bricks in a different pattern is an effective device, here coupled with a sculpted panel.

ON THE LINE (BELOW)
Tall lot-line fences can seem less imposing at a distance from the patio. Board-on-board designs are attractive on both sides, helping keep peace with the neighbors.

SEEING THROUGH IT
(ABOVE) Tempered-glass panels in steel frames keep the view open and enhance the modernistic lines of this contemporary design.

OPEN INVITATION
(BELOW) Front fences can mark property lines yet still provide a welcoming invitation to guests. Open patterns generally work best.

fences & walls

DOING IT ALL. Fences and walls enhance patio style, define spaces, and increase privacy. They mark property edges and create a distinctive identity. They also can provide a backdrop for decorative accents and screen unattractive views.

Walls can hold back a slope, creating level ground for a patio. And fences can contribute to outdoor comfort, taming strong winds into comforting breezes.

PLACE AND PURPOSE. Materials and location affect the style of a wall or fence. Front-yard fences define a property line and can provide overtures of welcome. Back fences may be solid and higher.

fencing
the wind

Contrary to intuition, a high, solid structure—even the sides of a house—will not protect your patio from the wind.

The physics of wind make it vault a solid structure and come down on its leeward side, creating as much or more havoc than if the wind were uncontained. If you're planning a fence or wall to calm the prevailing winds, build it so that it filters the wind. Fencing patterns that employ open spaces between the boards—basket weave and louvered, for example—work well. Use lattice panels or other open framework on top of walls to filter the winds, or design the wall with openings. Small windows in a wall create an interesting textural pattern and frame tantalizing glimpses of views beyond.

UNDEREXPOSURE (ABOVE) Keeping a fence from becoming a stockade is easier with upper sections designed as open structures. Here lattice and slats reduce potential monotony.

UNDERARCHING (BELOW) An outdoor living room is protected by brick and antiqued stucco walls. The arched opening leading to the house is faced with red brick.

PLANTED PASSAGE Vines and latticework can offer privacy when constructing other structures is impractical. Large openings in the latticework allow partial views to the outside.

amen

After you've considered the basics, it's ti[me]
your eyes and envision your perfect outd[oor]
include? A pool for swimming on hot day[s]
with warmth and ambience? A serene sp[a]
sun goes down? Now is the time to selec[t]
the patio you're planning fulfills your drea[ms]

FIRST CHOICES

(ABOVE) Selecting a pool or spa involves considering the size and shape of the pool as well as the patio materials that will border it.

planning for amenities

LISTING WISHES. Planning for patio amenities begins with a look at your wish list. Make sure that you have the list prioritized; most patio amenities will increase the total costs.

REFINEMENTS. Most amenities come in different price levels, so you need specific ideas about what you want and how much you can spend. For example, if you want meals prepared on your patio, do you need a fully equipped kitchen or a simple freestanding barbecue grill? Should your pool be an inground model or an aboveground installation? Do you want low-voltage lights or a line-voltage system? If a water feature is on your list, does that mean a flowing stream, a waterfall and koi pond, or a modest-size bubbling fountain?

You can add amenities later as you can afford them, but make decisions now about what you plan to install in the future. Then prepare the site for them as you build your patio. Run power and water lines. Have gas lines installed for the future outdoor kitchen. That way they'll be in place when you're ready to add the upgrades.

OPEN TO FLAME

(ABOVE) Including a fireplace or fire pit that's built into the patio requires careful planning before construction begins. Lighting placement is important for night use.

WATER FEATURE

(RIGHT) Three jugs create an imaginative fountain set on a bed of large river rocks. Plumbing for the spigots was built into the wall.

PATH LIGHTING (RIGHT) Low decorative fixtures are best for casting light directly on a walkway. These conventional path lights operate on a line-voltage system.

TINY AND BRIGHT (BELOW) Low-voltage lights may be mounted on columns or railings. In a yard that gets at least six hours of sun daily, solar fixtures are another option.

lighting

DAY AND NIGHT. With proper lighting the patio is an enjoyable place to gather after dark. In addition to lending ambience, outdoor fixtures provide security and may be used to illuminate patio surfaces, walkways, and stairs. The best lighting schemes combine uplighting, downlighting, and path lighting to ensure functional areas and decorative objects are illuminated from the best angles.

VOLTAGE OPTIONS. Electric lighting usually is operated through line-voltage systems that use a home's 120-volt AC power or through low-voltage lighting with power reduced by a transformer to 12 volts of direct current. Line-voltage wiring typically requires approval from a building inspector, but low-voltage lighting rarely requires inspection, is safer for outdoor use, and offers more options for fixture materials and styles. If your patio receives ample sunlight during the day, consider solar lights for soft lighting. Fireplaces and candles provide ambient light and help establish an intimate mood.

EASY ILLUMINATION Candles suspended from a chandelier provide a striking alternative to electric lighting.

LAMPLIGHT (ABOVE)
This carriage lamp
with a flame-tip bulb is
made to mount on any
surface. It's only one
of the many outdoor
fixtures designed to
contribute to a specific
design theme.

lighting techniques

A good lighting plan makes a big contribution to a patio. The effect depends on the fixtures and lighting techniques used.

Concealed fixtures cast light on an object without calling attention to the fixture itself. They're great for uplighting or downlighting objects you want to highlight. Kits are available for mounting lights on trees without harming the trees. Decorative fixtures mounted on stakes or walls cast diffuse light and function as accents. Use them to illuminate steps and floors. Always provide enough light to make the patio safe, especially on paths and at entries, steps, and changes of grade. Conversation areas feel more intimate with subtle lighting. Wire select fixtures to dimmer switches to vary the light level.

TRAVELING IN STYLE Path lighting makes walking safe at night, but fixtures can be stylish too. Solar units require no wiring and are manufactured in styles to fit even the most modern patio design.

temperature control

CONDITIONAL APPROVAL. Nature often fails to provide perfect conditions for outdoor enjoyment. On many occasions it takes only a little alteration to make a patio climate—especially its temperature—comfortable. Fans and heaters will keep temperature extremes from sending you indoors and can extend the useful life of your patio by weeks.

FANS AND HEATERS. Outdoor fans create breezes that may be absent on a hot day. Choose a ceiling-mount unit for general cooling or a freestanding model to generate more localized air currents. Fans also help disperse insects and smoke created by cooking. Be sure that the fan is rated for outdoor use and wired for multiple speeds. Some brands come with lights or attachments that provide a cooling mist from a water supply.

Outdoor heaters can raise the temperature in a 15- to 20-foot area by as much as 10 to 15 degrees, and they come in a variety of styles—portables, deck heaters, overheads, infrareds, spot heaters, and fan-assisted. After considering safety and efficiency, choose a heater by fuel type—kerosene, butane, propane, or natural gas.

HEATING UP (ABOVE)
An outdoor heater makes evenings spent outside comfortable. This one reflects the Asian design of the patio area.

GET COOL A pool house provides distinctive connections to the outdoors while boasting amenities worthy of inside spaces, including a ceiling-mount fan for cooling breezes.

Vintage tiles add detail to a Spanish-style stucco fireplace. A contractor needs to be consulted about fire retardation before finishes such as stucco are applied.

fireplaces & fire pits

WARMING TREND. Fireplaces lend warmth and intimacy to outdoor spaces. The same features important to indoor fireplaces are useful outdoors, including a hearth to safeguard against burning embers, andirons to hold logs in place, fire screens to contain sparks, and a damper to control the fire's draft. Some fireplaces even include a rotisserie or brick-lined warming oven for cooking. Whether you're using a prefabricated metal modular system or a site-built masonry unit, enlist a professional mason or contractor to build your fireplace.

THE PITS. If the funds or the space are insufficient for a fireplace, consider an inground fire pit built to resemble a campfire. Or purchase a portable fire pit or chiminea to create a similar effect.

fireplace
planning

Before building a fireplace into your patio plans, be sure to:

▶ **CHECK REGULATIONS.** Many communities have requirements for setbacks and construction as well as seasonal burning or air-quality rules. Arid, fire-prone areas may restrict outdoor fires altogether.

▶ **THINK PLACEMENT.** The location of your outdoor fireplace affects surrounding spaces. Use a fireplace to block unsightly views or draw attention to a special part of the yard. A fireplace may mark off a dining space close to the home or be situated farther out in the yard.

▶ **CHOOSE MATERIALS.** Whether you select masonry, firebrick, or another material for your fireplace, make certain its style will match the style of your home's exterior.

MOVABLE BLAZE (ABOVE) An easy alternative to a built-in fire pit, this portable version stands on metal legs to prevent overheating the patio and includes a cover to capture sparks.

BELOWGROUND (BELOW) A sunken, circular seating area provides a unique setting for fire and water. The water feature runs down the wall and into a small pond under the woodburning pit.

Most outdoor fireplaces are freestanding, but this one is built into a wall of the home. A screen ensures that hot sparks are contained.

STOREHOUSE (ABOVE) The style of storage space is as important as the style of any other design element. This delightful shed behind a white picket fence keeps garden tools out of sight and adds an eyecatching focal point.

IN THE DETAILS (LEFT) Little accents, such as these gourds and sprigs of herbs and blossoms, go a long way toward making simple storage devices more attractive.

storage

NEVER ENOUGH. Though you might minimize the need for outdoor storage when you're planning your patio, you'll soon wish you had more of this commodity. To get the jump on accumulated patio stuff, make a list of things you might keep there—trash containers, folding chairs, cushions and pillows, cooking tools, and magazines and papers. Once you start you'll find the list grows quickly. Then figure out where you want to put these things.

OUT OF SIGHT. Commercial storage units fashioned from cedar or redwood can make attractive additions to your patio as well as provide a lot of storage space in a single structure. As an alternative you may want to plan built-in seating, especially around the patio perimeter. Benches with lids for seating and cushions for comfort can store tablecloths and dining accessories—and possibly the cushions when not in use. In spaces used for entertaining, such built-ins are great for folding chairs and, when equipped with lift-out trays, can stow large quantities of partyware.

Small containers work too—antique canisters for pet foods, decorated mailboxes for reading material, rolling racks for odds and ends. And of course all these portable compartments increase your collection of decorative accents.

BIN THERE (BELOW) Hiding trash containers becomes an easy enterprise with an attractive enclosure such as this. It's constructed of low-cost materials and gets its Craftsman style from simple details, such as the small openings and inverted post caps.

SMART LEDGE (BELOW) Raising a sunken spa slightly keeps pets and people from falling into the water. The ledge also serves as a resting spot for guests and beverages.

pools & spas

UNIFYING ELEMENTS. Patios make great borders for swimming pools and spas. In addition to ensuring that there's plenty of room for moving and lounging around water amenities, patios help pools and spas blend with the surrounding landscape. Avoid a haphazard look by relying on a unifying aesthetic. All parts of the design—including the patio, pool, and house—should share the same or similar shapes and details and express the same architectural style.

CHOICES, CHOICES. Choose a pool or spa's shape and size to fit your budget and the site. Pools and spas may be located above or below the ground and may be prefabricated or custom-made. Consider maintenance when selecting materials for the patio and water amenities. Most patio materials are durable, but some are safer and better-suited for use near water than others.

Contemplate location as well. Plan for access to electrical and plumbing systems and equipment such as water heaters and filters—particularly for inground amenities. If possible locate the pool and spa in a place that takes advantage of views, offers privacy, provides sun or shade as needed, and is close to the house.

ALL IN ONE (ABOVE) Many pools are designed with a built-in spa. In this backyard, the brick spa flows into a tranquil blue pool. The nearby brick patio offers a place for lounging.

FLOATING PATIO
Elevating the patio a few feet above the pool lends a dramatic presence to this space. Multiple levels of plantings and hardscaping make a small pool area seem larger.

POOLSIDE LOUNGING (ABOVE) Chaise longues provide a spot for catching some rays next to a lap pool. The wooden fence offers privacy and meets building codes that require childproof fences and gates around pools.

pool & spa
patio safety

Avoid pool and spa mishaps by taking the proper measures from the moment you begin planning your patio.

When selecting patio surfaces, avoid slick materials such as glazed ceramic tile and polished marble, which are safety hazards when wet. Also stay away from surfaces such as dark slate pavers that absorb heat readily and may burn feet. Find out whether local building codes require childproof fences and gates around pools and plan accordingly. And make certain to reserve a spot on a wall or fence near the pool for lifesaving devices.

WITHIN LIMITS Even a small backyard can accommodate a pool. Curved profiles, such as the one featured in this kidney-shape pool, add a casual dimension to a rectangular space.

A CURRENT EVENT (ABOVE) By employing the same materials throughout, this patio creates a unified space that allows the spa to blend comfortably into its surroundings and avoid appearing as an individual element.

GATHER 'ROUND (BELOW) With privacy from a fence panel, this whirlpool surrounded by ferns and flowering plants creates a world of its own for family and friends.

SHORTFALLS Ponds and waterfalls should match the scale of the landscape. Even a small water feature such as this provides a pleasant distraction, and the dark rocks help set it off from the white limestone borders.

fountains & ponds

MAGIC MOMENTS. Fountains and ponds add tranquility to outdoor spaces. A sparkle of light catches the eye, and the sound of water is soothing and masks distracting noises.

Options for fountains and ponds mean design opportunities. Fountains are made as freestanding or wall-mount units and come in many materials and styles. Spray patterns are design elements too.

Ponds can take on the outline of preformed liners, or you can shape your own with a flexible liner. When planning a pond check whether local codes place safety restrictions on installations.

LEVELS OF ATTENTION (RIGHT) With its waterfall issuing from the middle of the wall, this installation creates a powerful impression. Multiple levels add to its interest and the soothing sounds it provides.

TIER DROPS A three-tiered fountain enclosed by a low wrought-iron fence acts as the centerpiece for this brick-lined courtyard. Water spills from each level in a quiet trickle.

EUROPEAN UNION

(ABOVE) A two-tier fountain with lion's-head spouts, statuary, urns, and a broken concrete walkway work together to create a backyard of old-world ambience.

MODERN MONOLITHS (LEFT)

Cast in heavy rectangular forms, poured concrete creates this clean, contemporary waterfall. Small statuary perched on the steps adds a humorous touch that lightens the visual weight of the installation.

BRIMMING OVER

(ABOVE) Resting on a concrete base and rising quietly from the lily pond, this ornate fountain introduces a vertical element that breaks up the horizontal expanse of a large side yard.

easy **enhancements**

Amenities needn't be large, expensive enterprises. Sometimes simple elements have great impact.

Wind chimes add a therapeutic sound, an instantly soothing antidote to hectic days. Install one or two in different sizes and made from different materials for a range of sounds. Weatherproof speakers can bring your favorite music outdoors. A radio-frequency remote control will let you change programs without leaving your seat. Even if you have little need for an outdoor symphony, install electric outlets for your laptop computer and other conveniences and a hookup for the cordless phone. Fragrances create their own aura as they waft over a patio. Plant flowers with your favorite scents. Lilacs, roses, and peonies are a few good choices.

outdoor kitchens

Outdoor kitchens have become fixtures of modern living. Certainly you can get along without one—but what's the fun in that? Besides there's something singular about an outdoor dining experience whether it's an intimate dinner for two, a frolicking family meal, or a large feast for your monthly party crowd.

planning a kitchen layout

STEELING AWAY (LEFT) Food preparation, cooking, storage, and dining space are close at hand in this installation. The white ashlar wall allows the stainless-steel grill to fit in seamlessly.

CUISINE QUIZ. Planning an outdoor kitchen begins with questions. Which type of cooking will you do? How many people will you cook for? How frequently will you cook outdoors? Your answers will help you identify how much space and which appliances you'll need. Maybe you need only a grill. Perhaps a full kitchen with a griddle, side burners, refrigerator, sinks, and storage is in order.

Next decide where to situate the kitchen. A location close to the interior kitchen can make cooking outdoors convenient and cut installation costs, but a freestanding kitchen can make a great addition to a detached patio or pool.

MAIN ATTRACTION
(LEFT) This fireplace, grill, and sink assembled in a horseshoe layout extend the living area into the outdoors. Slate pavers cut to fit the edges of an existing slab create the right amount of extra space for the outdoor kitchen.

cooking
safely

No matter where you locate your outdoor kitchen, be sure that you've picked a safe spot.

If your outdoor cooking facility is a simple roll-out grill, place it away from flammable materials and out of main traffic routes. Your grill also needs to be out from under overhangs, awnings, other flammable structures, and tree branches. Include a freestanding fan in your plans to send cooking smoke away from guests.

A built-in installation should conform to all fire-safety measures mandated by local building codes. Both exterior and interior materials need to be fireproof, and woodframe construction should include insulating, nonflammable material between hot surfaces and the frame. Have all electrical appliances grounded to prevent shock, and protect electrical circuits with ground fault circuit interrupter outlets.

Protect your outdoor kitchen by using waterproof materials or coverings. And always keep a freshly charged fire extinguisher on hand.

KITCHEN HELP Even a fully equipped outdoor kitchen such as this—outfitted with side burners and a prep sink— benefits by a location close to the kitchen inside the house.

THE REAL DEAL

(LEFT) When space and budget allow, a kitchen that includes a prep sink, a grill and side burner, an undercounter refrigerator, and counter space provides the ultimate outdoor cooking experience.

MODEST SERVING (BELOW) A well-equipped kitchen, complete with shaded dining space, draws guests outdoors in all but the most inclement weather. Using stone in the base unit continues the natural design theme set by the flagstone patio.

materials

DESIGN EXTENSION. Begin your selection by looking at your house. A kitchen close to the house should complement its style, using the same or similar materials.

A MATERIAL DIFFERENCE. Almost any material used in an indoor kitchen may be used outdoors—if it's protected. For example, properly finished wood cabinets would be suitable in a gazebo.

Weatherproof materials such as teak, stainless steel, brick, stone, cedar, tile, and stucco take weather worries out of construction. (Stainless steel is best kept covered when not in use.)

Stainless steel, stone, and tile make suitable countertops, but consider advantages and disadvantages. Metal tends to be noisy. Some stone is too uneven, while others are too soft or susceptible to staining. Your tile choice needs to withstand the elements. Formed concrete is a good choice for a countertop because it's hardy and lends itself to an array of contours.

MAKING THE CURVE (ABOVE) A curved layout brings kitchen work centers close to one another without making the space feel confined. Brick and concrete conform easily to this curved design.

REMAINING NEUTRAL (BELOW) Concrete goes with anything. Its neutral gray keeps competition with other colors to a minimum. Concrete also can be colored to complement other design schemes.

appliances & fixtures

CENTER STAGE. The grill is the centerpiece of an outdoor kitchen, and the features you include will depend on the meals you will prepare most often. Steak and vegetables need a hot grill. For broiled fowl, add a rotisserie; sausage and eggs need a griddle. Meals for large groups will be easier with more burners and a side unit. You may want to add a fryer and a smoker. Natural gas is the most convenient fuel, but liquid propane is the most common. Of course a basic setup might include a charcoal grill.

FOR BIGGER BANQUETS. Depending on your needs and budget, you may add other appliances and accessories to your kitchen. Substantial outdoor kitchens need storage for dry foods, pots and pans, cooking utensils, and dinnerware.

An undercounter refrigerator and prep sink are usually the next choices. A prep sink lets you fill pots, clean produce, and rinse dishes. Elaborate outdoor kitchens might include a dishwasher.

SPOUTING OFF (BELOW) Fixtures, such as this copper sink and copper faucet, should be chosen with as much attention to style as interior fixtures. Quality fixtures will last for years before needing maintenance.

COOKING WITH GAS Grills equipped with multiple heating elements allow precise control for foods requiring different temperatures. Enough counterspace to provide a "landing" for hot utensils is a must.

SIDEKICK (ABOVE)
The addition of a side burner greatly expands outdoor culinary options. Most models include a weatherproof cover to protect the unit when it's not in use.

OPENING OPTIONS
(LEFT) Rotisseries and smokers are optional conveniences offered with some grill models. The space under the unit may be used to house propane tanks or to store items.

COMPACT COOKING
(ABOVE) This kitchen includes all the outdoor cooking essentials—grill, cooktop, prep sink, and undercounter storage—in a compact space. A glazed-tile mural adds a decorative touch.

MADE TO ORDER (LEFT) For morning breakfast nothing beats the convenience of a griddle. Downdraft units will keep the smoke out of the eyes of the cook and guests.

style

Style will greatly affect how often you use your outdoor living space. Build a plain patio and you're likely to find it unused. Build a stylish model, one that expresses your personality and taste, and you will want to stay outdoors. The key is to find the right combination of landscaping, furnishings, and accessories to convey the style you choose.

planning for style

GET PERSONAL. If there's any secret to creating an alluring patio style, it's to use colors, furnishings, amenities, and accents that result in a setting that reflects your personality.

HARMONIOUS UNITY. Continuity with the style of the house is important for a patio located close to it. So is harmony. Using the same or similar materials will help achieve both. Pick up a detail from a molding and include it on the pergola. Paint an arbor the color of the trim. Align the patio with the orientation of the house. Use angles in the paving next to a modern home, bric-a-brac with a Victorian setting.

Elements outside the patio provide a setting for it and play a role in defining style. Flowerbeds, paths, edgings, walls, and fireplaces all contribute to a sense of style. The lines of the adjacent landscaping should mirror the curves, straight lines, or angles of the patio. Once you have planned the architectural details of the space, finish it off with furnishings and decorative accents, varying the shapes, colors, and textures of these items throughout the setting.

ALL LINED UP (BELOW) Symmetry defines this formal space, and accents continue the theme. As wisteria weaves through the lattice, it creates an interesting counterpoint in this Georgian bower.

DESIGN THEMES. Style themes group elements to reflect a specific region, historical period, ethnicity, or heritage. Most style themes fall generally into either formal or informal categories. Formal styles are marked by symmetry. Informal styles seem more natural and casual.

Regional themes pick up elements that are specific to a geographical area and build around them. It may be handmade tiles surrounded by cactus, sand, and rock creating a Southwestern theme or bonsai plantings and a Zen garden for an Asian-style patio.

Historical themes capitalize on colors, lines, textures, and patterns used in a specific time period. A Victorian theme would employ multiple colors in ornate wood structures and paving with formal lines. A contemporary theme might feature strong angles, straight lines, the use of empty space as a design element, and a monochromatic color theme.

STUDY IN CONTRASTS Partnered with a collection of right-angle forms throughout and the dark contrast of the cushions on light wicker, the carved Indonesian screen balances the rectangular window frames and conjures a style with a hint of far-off places.

COMELY COURTYARD

(LEFT) Lavish layers of detail create an old-world ambience in this courtyard. Aged brick walls, luxurious draperies, ornate statuary, and an Italianate dining set all contribute to the theme of this courtyard patio.

POSITIVE REACTION

(BELOW) Negative space creates a positive reaction in contemporary design. Wide glass panels, open soffits, and concrete slabs are softened by the grass and manicured shrubs.

FROM THE AREA Local stone, plants, and materials help create a regional theme for this patio. Local materials are also less costly, and plants grow well in their native climate.

REINFORCEMENTS (RIGHT)
The small pergola above the fence is more decorative than functional, but it helps unify the space by mirroring the larger pergola overhead. River rock provides a weighty anchor without intruding.

FAR-EAST FLING
(BELOW) Loose fabric draped from an arched portico and netting hung from the ceiling create a private Arabian-theme retreat. The fabric may be tied together for privacy.

finding
your style

Use this simple method to help you discover your design style.

Look around your neighborhood at other patio designs. Make notes about what you like and don't like—color combinations, how the patio relates to its surroundings, materials, patterns. Let your instincts guide you. Keep these notes in a folder. Study landscape magazines and clip photos of things that appeal to you. Put these in the folder too. Then go through the folder and discard what you no longer like. Look through what's left and you'll begin to notice patterns and consistencies. Those are the foundations of your style.

CONTINUING SAGA (ABOVE) Nothing provides a unifying stylistic element like a continuity of material. Here the use of brick on the floor is continued on the ledges and fireplace structure.

CHECKERBOARD (BELOW) Unglazed brick tiles set in sand and interspaced with colored gravel create a display of alternating textures that activates this patio floor. Similar fabric colors extend the theme.

patterns & textures

THE RIGHT TOUCH. Materials possess a particular texture, smooth or rough, soft or hard. Repeated materials create patterns. Regular patterns lend stability to the design, while random patterns create energy and interest. Texture and pattern come together in patio paving.

HOW YOU SEE IT. Natural stone may impart a rustic or classic quality. With contrasting mortar joints the shape of the stones predominates; with a matching joint color, the focus is on the overall shape of the patio. With bricks texture is secondary to pattern. Its patterns can alter the perception of the length and width of the patio. Tile comes in a variety of shapes and colors that can generate a multitude of compositions. Concrete is smooth in its natural state but can be roughened or fully patterned.

TONING IT DOWN Although the running bond brick pattern looks stately, the expanse of the walls is softened by creeping vines and the vertical bricks bordering the top. On the paving crushed stone becomes a playful foil between the limestone slabs.

ECCENTRICITIES (ABOVE) An erratic pattern in the stone walls of the fireplace is anchored by the brick hearth. The varied colors of the materials heighten the visual play and textural contrast.

THE MASTER'S HAND (BELOW) Differently sized stone adds to the handhewn character of this fireplace. Such unplanned looks are best achieved by sketching patterns first.

A SQUARE DEAL Vertical lines and multitextured objects abound in this design, but the predominant colors and patterns of the tile floor help to anchor the space and give the eye a place to rest.

landscaping

UNIFICATION DEVICE. A patio is one element in a larger landscape rather than an individual entity. Landscaping provides an excellent way to integrate your patio with the rest of the yard.

USEFUL ARTISTRY. Plants sculpt the landscape, emphasizing or softening the borders of a patio. They can define the limits of the patio or lead the eye to the landscape beyond. Hide an unattractive view with hedges. Small trees in containers provide portable privacy. Direct traffic by creating walkways between container plantings.

Pick plants whose blooming coincides with the season in which you'll use the patio. If you would rather relax than tend to plants, select varieties that need little attention. Choose species that thrive in your climate and avoid varieties whose mature height will overwhelm the patio.

DOWN IN FRONT

(RIGHT) Growing plants in tiers, with the lowest at the front and the tallest toward the back, lets every species display its own individuality. It also provides a colorful enclosure that marks this patio area as a special place.

COBBLED TOGETHER (RIGHT)
Cobblestones set the tone for this landscaped patio, while the explosion of foliage texture provides ongoing interest and beckons guests to other sections of the garden.

LIGHTEN UP (ABOVE) Tall foliage along the back of the planting bed breaks up the dark louvered privacy-fence sections and, with the other plantings, helps brighten this pool deck.

GETTING AN EYEFUL Diverse containers, a window box, and unusual molded planters make the walk past the window to the door a playful journey.

POTSHOT (RIGHT) It's usually best to keep the style of a container garden in the same vein as the overall style of the outdoor space. Standard clay pots create a cottage garden atmosphere, but an ornamental urn such as this works best in a formal setting.

OASIS ACCENTS

(ABOVE) Flowerbeds possess multiple design possibilities. Here raised beds and low-growing plants in curved perimeters accent the horizontal plane of the pool deck.

TANTALIZING JOURNEY (LEFT) With its entrance defined by small plants in containers, this path is dotted with plantings that keep the journey interesting.

CLASSICALLY TRAINED The contours of the planting beds define the edges of the hardscape on this loose rock and flagstone patio. Mixed plantings offer season-long visual interest.

PUSHING THE PALETTE (LEFT) One of the great advantages of container gardens is that they can be moved to suit the view, the size of the patio, and the function the patio provides.

container
gardens

Even if you're planning a landscape scheme that features a variety of planting beds, remember the appeal of container gardens.

Just about anything will grow in containers, and that's only the start of their versatility. You can move them around to keep the arrangement surprising, dress up empty spots on the patio, hide unattractive views, or even create a view where one is lacking. Plant the same species or color in containers as those in the flowerbeds and bring the landscape right onto the patio. Add privacy or shade with tall potted shrubs, and create floating compositions with a careful arrangement of planted baskets. Plant a series of containers throughout the growing season to ensure that something is always in bloom.

SIMPLE DETAILS
(RIGHT) A durable teak table and chairs adorned with striped cushions are perfect for an outdoor dining area. The white umbrella adds timeless style and provides shade.

LOUNGING AROUND (BELOW)
Furnishings should look inviting and feel comfortable. These handsome cushioned chaise longues beckon for a relaxing afternoon outdoors.

furnishings

SETTLING IN. Choosing furnishings is more than picking things to sit on. They help organize space and provide a place from which to relax and enjoy your patio.

Furniture choices should strike a balance between comfort and style. First select several options based on a look you like. Certain designs evoke certain styles—intricate wrought iron feels Victorian, while sleek powder-coated metals suggest contemporary. Sit on chairs to determine whether they're comfortable. If possible purchase dining and lounging furnishings from the same style line to have consistency of style.

Practicality also should guide your choices. You'll want durable, weatherproof frames and fabrics. If you'll rearrange frequently choose a style that's easy to move. Also select furnishings in a scale appropriate to your patio size.

SINGULAR ACHIEVEMENT
Several groupings of furniture from the same style line lend continuity to this multifunctional patio space.

NO FUSS (ABOVE) A simple cedar dining set creates a relaxing spot for informal dining or gazing at the water in the bay. Some woods, such as cedar, are naturally resistant to harsh weather.

ROUGH AND READY
Rustic handmade
furniture provides a
one-of-a-kind addition
to a patio. Such pieces
look wonderful against
a backdrop of greenery.

CLASSIC COMFORT The comfort of Adirondack chairs is indisputable. Here they make a perfect spot for taking in the beauty of the garden bordering the patio.

DECORATIVE DETAIL (BELOW) Details in the construction and design of fabric-covered items, such as this bolster's gathered and buttoned swirl, add pleasant elements that enhance the style of a patio.

fabrics: design & durability

You want a fabric that enhances the style of your patio. But maintenance and durability also should be high on the list.

Look for solution-dyed fabrics that feature colors integral to the fabric. They resist fading and sun damage, stand up to rigorous use, and are virtually stainproof. Acrylic and olefin fabrics usually are solution-dyed. If you're in the market for cushioned furniture, ask about brands that release moisture. Open-celled foam materials such as polyester fiberfill let moisture pass through so the fabrics last longer than materials that trap moisture.

FROM THE BOTTOM UP (LEFT) Fluted urns on the paver floor and the small section of stained-glass window are details that add an interesting touch to this greenhouse getaway.

decorating with accents

TAKE YOUR PICK. Accents provide the spice in outdoor design. Use them as focal points or as ornaments. Almost anything can become an accent—collections of objects, old tools, statuary, pottery, even interesting stones or driftwood.

NESTING PLACES. Start decorating your patio after all other aspects are complete. This gives you a chance to sit in various areas of your patio and take stock of its appearance. Look for bare spots that could use a little pizzazz. If the space needs a structure to hold an ornament, fasten shelves to walls and fences or bring in a pedestal, antique stool, or a vintage garden-style chair. Make sure you have at least one focal point for every sitting vantage point, but don't overwhelm an area by putting objects too close together. The competition for attention will prove annoying. Artful wire forms, metal sculptures, topiaries, and espaliers make interesting focal points and will help draw you out to your patio, where you can relax and enjoy them.

SUN DISK (LEFT) Hanging a medallion on a fireplace adds an accent that breaks up the vertical line of the chimney. Such accents must be chosen so their size is proportionate to their surroundings.

FILLING IN (ABOVE) Almost anything can be an accent. Here the vase, china chicken, and lantern make the bare space on the countertop a little more interesting.

NEW WINE (LEFT) Why toss an old galvanized washtub when a coat of paint can transform it into a decorative and useful objet d'art?

SWING SHIFT. Although this structure is made primarily to support the swing, it shows that thinking only slightly outside the box can turn a strictly functional object into a dramatic focal point.

INSIDE OR OUT? (LEFT) It's hard to tell that this stunning setup, with its stylish furnishings, chandelier, fireplace, flat-screen television, and built-in shelves, is actually a patio area.

RECLAMATION (BELOW) Hanging pots fastened to an old ornamental fence section are a great way to display flowering plants.

contact information

The Home Depot® offers patio and garden products and materials from major manufacturers either in stock or through special order. This extensive inventory offers customers a comprehensive and varied selection that will ensure a patio that truly reflects their personal style and taste while enabling them to stick to a realistic budget. Information on products and materials may be obtained from Home Depot stores or directly through manufacturers by mail, telephone, or online.

Contacting Meredith Corporation
To order this and other Meredith Corporation books call 800/678-8091. For further information about the information contained in this book, please contact specific manufacturers and professionals or contact Meredith by e-mail at hi123@mdp.com or by phone at 800/678-2093.

Contacting the Home Depot
For general information about product availability, contact your local Home Depot or visit The Home Depot® website at www.homedepot.com.

professionals

Listed are the names and contact information for the professionals who worked on the new patio locations shot exclusively for The Home Depot® that are featured in this book.

5, 26–27, 66 (bottom), 95 (top):
Field Editor—Elaine St. Louis
Photographer—Emily Minton Redfield
Landscape Architect—Jerry Nelson, Nelson Design, Greeley, CO

8–11, 79 (top):
Field Editor—Leigh Elmore
Photographer—Kim Golding
Landscape Architect—Merle Brown, Connexions, LLC, 13250 W. 98 St., Lenexa, KS 66215; 913/871-5100; 9138715101@myconnexions.net

12–13, 102 (bottom):
Field Editor—Shirley Remes
Photographer—Kritsada Panichgul
Landscape Contractor—Plandscape, Inc., 707 E. North St., Elburn, IL 60119; 630/365-2558; www.plandscapeinc.com

14–15, 69, 84 (top right), 100 (top), 105 (bottom), 152, 168 (bottom), 176 (bottom):
Field Editor—Karin Lidbeck Brent
Photographer—Michael Partenio
Landscape Designer—Jessica Livingston, Jessica Livingston Landscape & Floral Design; 203/637-1965; jessicaliv@hotmail.com

16–19:
Field Editor—Elaine St. Louis
Photographer—Linda Hanselman
Interior Designer—Lane Elizabeth Oliver Interior Design, Inc., 881 S. York St., Denver, CO 80209; 303/722-4288; www.leointeriordesign.com; lane@leointeriors.com

20–21, 78, 124, 154 (bottom):
Field Editor—Lisa Mowry
Photographer—Emily Followill
Interior Designer—Melanie Millner, The Design Atelier; 404/365-8662; melanie@thedesignatelier.com

22–23, 77 (bottom), 81 (top left):
Field Editor—Elaine St. Louis
Photographer—J. Curtis Photography
Architect—Stephen Sparn Architects, PC Planning and Design, 1731 15 St., Ste. 250, Boulder, CO 80302; 303/442-4422; www.sparn.com

Landscape Architect—Richelle Reilly, Greenstreets, 1526 Spruce St., Ste. 230, Boulder, CO 80302; 303/443-9680

24–25, 106 (top), 183 (bottom):
Photographer—Dana Wheelock
No professional information available.

28–31:
Field Editor—Elaine St. Louis
Photographer—Emily Minton Redfield
Interior Designer—Lane Elizabeth Oliver Interior Design, Inc., 881 S. York St., Denver, CO 80209; 303/722-4288; www.leointeriordesign.com; lane@leointeriors.com

34–35:
Field Editor—Elaine St. Louis
Photographer—Linda Hanselman
No professional information available.

36–37, 83 (top left), 111 (bottom):
Field Editor—Elaine St. Louis
Photographer—Povy Kendal Atchison
No professional information available.

38–39, 81 (top right), 142 (top):
Field Editor—Linda Humphrey
Photographer—Mike Jensen
No professional information available.

42, 47 (top), 92 (top left), 178:
Field Editor—Loralee Wenger
Photographer—Mike Jensen
No professional information available.

43 (top), 50 (left), 77 (top), 139 (bottom), 150 (top), 172, 180, 181 (bottom):
Field Editor—Andrea Caughey
Photographer—Ed Gohlich
Kitchen Designer—Kristin Victor Design, 2305 India St., San Diego, CA 92101; 619/696-1068
Landscape Contractor—H.A. Casillas Landscape & Construction, 3498 Wallace Dr., Bonita, CA 91902; 619/267-1343

44, 108 (top), 140 (top), 146 (bottom):
Field Editor—Shirley Remes
Photographer—Kritsada Panichgul
Landscape Architect—Plandscape, Inc., 707 E. North St., Elburn, IL 60119; 630/365-2558; www.plandscapeinc.com

46, 52 (bottom), 91 (bottom), 175 (bottom):
Field Editor—Leigh Elmore
Photographer—Kim Golding
No professional information available.

47 (bottom), 71, 90:
Field Editor—Shirley Remes
Photographer—Julie Sprott
No professional information available.

49 (top and bottom left), 53 (top and bottom), 92 (middle), 115 (top), 140 (bottom), 158 (top):
Field Editor—Andrea Caughey
Photographer—Ed Gohlich
Architect—House & Dodge Design Inc., 2100 Fourth Ave., San Diego, CA 92101; 619/557-0575; www.houseanddodge.com
Landscape Architect—Jeffrey Rule Inc., Landscape Architect, 8080 La Mesa Blvd., Ste. 206, La Mesa, CA 91941; 619/466-0362; www.jeffreyrule.com

Builder—Scott Carter, Brookline Homes, 650 S. Cherry St., Ste 205, Denver, CO 80246; 303/388-6222; www.brooklinecolorado.com
Architect—Godden/Sudik Architects, 6025 S. Quebec St., Ste. 375, Centennial, CO 80111; 303/455-4437; www.goddensudik.com
Interior Designer—Kristen Schmidt, Amirob & Associates, 1948 Blake St., Denver, CO 80202; 303/296-7388; www.amirob.com
Landscape Architect—Owens Landscape Design and Management, Inc., 19035 E. Plaza Dr., Parker, CO 80134; 303/843-9629; owenslandscape@aol.com

102 (top), 146 (top), 150 (bottom), 153 (top and bottom), 181 (top):
Field Editor—Sunday Hendrickson
Photographer—Mark Lohman
Landscape Architect—Mark Berry, Pasadena, CA
Landscape Contractor—Hackman's Landscape Service; 626/355-4664

155 (top), 185 (left):
Field Editor—Elaine St. Louis
Photographer—Emily Minton Redfield
Builder—Cayd Bader, Berkshire Homes, 680 W. 121 Ave., Ste. 130, Westminster, CO 80234; 303/457-1313; www.theberkshirelife.com
Architect—Knudson Gloss Architects, 820 Riverbend Rd., Boulder, CO 80301; 303/442-5882; www.kgarch.com
Interior Designer—Jane V. Gates-Raile, IIDA, Interior Settings, LLC; 303/985-1980; jraile@interiorsettings.com

166 (top), 182 (bottom):
Field Editor—Andrea Caughey
Photographer—Ed Gohlich
Architect—Al Saroyan II, AIA, 710 Redwood Ave., Sand City, CA 93955; 831/393-1800

171 (top):
Field Editor—Peggy Keonjian
Photographer—Laurie Black
Garden and Structure Design and Construction—Les Bugajski, Sunbox Designs, 2601 N.E. 86 Ave., Vancouver, WA 98662; 360/254-7087; mbug4@comcast.net

108 (bottom), 112, 149 (bottom), 183 (top), 184:
Field Editor—Andrea Caughey
Photographer—Ed Gohlich
Contractor—Dan Avis, Dan Avis Construction, 1364 Justin Rd., Cardiff, CA 92007; 858/395-4602

index

a-b

c

d-f

g-l